The Waiting

How God Works While We Wait

DEBBIE BARR

AspirePress

The Mystery of Waiting:
How God Works While We Wait

Copyright © 2024 Deborah Barr
Published by Aspire Press
An imprint of Tyndale House Ministries
Carol Stream, Illinois
www.hendricksonrose.com

ISBN: 978-1-4964-8361-4

All rights reserved. No part of this book may be reproduced or transmitted in any form or by any means, electronic or mechanical, including photocopying, recording, or by any information storage and retrieval system, without permission in writing from the publisher.

The views and opinions expressed in this book are those of the author(s) and do not necessarily express the views of Tyndale House Ministries or Aspire Press, nor is this book intended to be a substitute for mental health treatment or professional counseling. The information in this resource is intended as a guideline for healthy living. Please consult qualified medical, legal, pastoral, and psychological professionals regarding individual concerns. Tyndale House Ministries and Aspire Press are in no way liable for any content, change of content, or activity for the works listed. Citation of a work does not mean endorsement of all its contents or of other works by the same author.

All Scripture quotations, unless otherwise indicated, are taken from the Holy Bible, New International Version,® NIV.® Copyright ©1973, 1978, 1984, 2011 by Biblica, Inc.® Used by permission of Zondervan. All rights reserved worldwide. www.zondervan.com. The "NIV" and "New International Version" are trademarks registered in the United States Patent and Trademark Office by Biblica, Inc.®

Author photo by Melinda Lamm. Cover photo: PHOTOCREO Michal Bednarek/Shutterstock.com. Other images used under license from Shutterstock.com.

Printed in the United States of America
010424VP

Contents

INTRODUCTION
Waiting 5

CHAPTER 1
In the Waiting Room 7

CHAPTER 2
If You're Waiting, God Is Working 39

CHAPTER 3
The Mystery of Waiting... 77

AFTERWORD
A Personal Note..101

Resources 103

Introduction
Waiting

WAITING IS HARD.

No one is a fan of waiting. Yet, waiting is a universal experience. We've all waited. We've waited for big things: for the baby to be born, for the chemotherapy to end, to find out—*did I get the job?*, for the soldier to come home, for the house to sell, for the prodigal to return, for answers to our prayers. We've all waited for little things too: for fish to bite, for the plane to take off, for our turn in the checkout line, for the traffic jam to clear.

Though no one likes to wait, waiting is just part of life. More importantly, it's also part of God's plan for every life. That's why waiting is a bit of a mystery. *Why does God make us wait? Why, when it would be so easy for God to just say "yes," does he instead so often say "wait"? What can waiting teach us about God? Can the experience of waiting change us?* You'll find answers to these questions—and plenty to think about—on the pages ahead. The truth is, whenever you are in a season of waiting, God is working in ways you can't see.

If this book could have a soundtrack, it would be the song "Waiting Here for You." This beautiful song about waiting on God is a fitting prelude to the chapters ahead. If you search for this song on YouTube, you'll find inspiring performances by Christy Nockels, Melodie Malone, and other gifted vocalists. Listen and be blessed.

Chapter 1
In the Waiting Room

WAITING. IT SOUNDS SO SIMPLE, EVEN RELAXING, doesn't it? Just sitting in a comfy chair, maybe flipping through a magazine, until the thing you're waiting for happens. If you're waiting for your hair appointment or getting your tires rotated, that's a pretty good definition of waiting. But if you've ever spent a day anxiously awaiting updates in a surgical waiting room or trying to renew your driver's license at the DMV without an appointment, you know that not all waiting experiences are relaxing. Depending on what you're waiting for, even one day of waiting can seem unbearably long and emotionally draining (*They haven't updated me for two hours! What if the surgery isn't going well?*). And if the waiting room is overcrowded and hot, you might be physically uncomfortable too, especially if you got there after all the comfy chairs were taken.

While spending the day in a waiting room is no one's idea of fun, it's an easy assignment compared to situations that keep us waiting for weeks, months, or even years. Prolonged waiting can try one's patience as nothing else can. It's like sitting at a traffic light that seems to be permanently stuck on red. You want to get on with things! But you cannot. You're "on hold," unable to change your circumstances. Despite your best efforts, you can't close the gap between your present reality and the change you yearn for.

Welcome to the waiting room.

What Does the Bible Say About Waiting?

You might be surprised to know that the Bible has a lot to say about waiting. In most translations, the words *wait, waited,* or *waiting* appear more than one hundred times. Waiting is encouraged and modeled for us in dozens of verses and mentioned over and over in different contexts. The sheer number of times the Bible mentions waiting flags it as something important, something God wants us to pay special attention to.

In newer translations of the Bible, Psalm 27:14 tells us to "wait *for* the Lord." In the King James and other older versions, this verse tells us to wait *on* the Lord. Whether we think of it as waiting *on*, waiting *for*, or even waiting *upon* the Lord, the idea is that we're depending on him to guide us while we're in the waiting room.

> "The Lord is good to those who wait for him,
> to the soul who seeks him."
> LAMENTATIONS 3:25 ESV

What Does It Mean to Wait on God?

Waiting for the Lord is different from other kinds of waiting, like waiting to be seated at a restaurant or waiting to feel a tug on your fishing line. When we think of waiting on God, we typically think in terms of waiting for him to answer our prayers. As God's children, we speak to our Father in prayer, telling him our desires and our problems, and making our requests. Then we wait, trusting that he will respond. This, most definitely, is waiting on God, and it is our privilege as God's children to do so. However, when we tell God our wants and needs and ask him to meet them, what matters most to him is the attitude of our heart.

> Waiting on God means we seek his perfect timing and guidance before making big decisions or big commitments.

For some people, waiting on God is like waiting for an Amazon delivery: they place an order and expect God to fill it. Their plan, not God's plan, is most in focus. This is not what it means to wait on God!

Waiting on God means we come to him as our Father, not just asking for what we want, but asking him what *he* wants *for us*. It means asking him to fulfill our desires and solve our problems, not according to our short-sighted human plans, but in ways that fulfill his perfect plan for our lives. Waiting on God means we seek his perfect timing and guidance before making big decisions or big commitments. Bottom line, waiting on God means that we really believe that his plan for our lives is best—and that his best is worth waiting for.

But what if we're not really sure about all of this? How can we wait on God if we're not sure he really has the power to answer our prayers or cares enough to intervene in our lives?

The Sovereignty of God

How confidently we wait on God—or whether we wait on him at all—hinges upon what we believe about his sovereignty.

We know that Moses, Isaiah, Jeremiah, David, Simeon, Gideon, and the martyrs in the book of Revelation all believed that God is sovereign. We know this because when they spoke to him, they called him Sovereign Lord. The word *sovereign* means, as the psalmist described, that God "does whatever pleases him, in the heavens and on the earth, in the seas and all their depths" (Psalm 135:6). There is no higher authority, no more ultimate power than our sovereign God. Yet this highest authority tenderly loves and deeply cares for people, which inspires awe and gratitude in those who know him, as is evident in this verse:

> Then King David went in and sat before the Lord, and he said: "Who am I, Sovereign Lord, and what is my family, that you have brought me this far?... How great you are, Sovereign Lord! There is no one like you, and there is no God but you."
>
> 2 SAMUEL 7:18, 22

Because the Lord is sovereign and all-knowing (omniscient), his knowledge of you is perfect. He foreknew every day of your life before even one of them had occurred (Psalm 139:16). This means he also foresaw the needs and problems that make you pray or cry, and the reasons for your waiting now. There's no circumstance or problem you're facing, or will ever face, that will cause him to say, "Wow, I didn't see *that* coming!" If the thought of that makes you laugh, then you recognize God's sovereignty. He's sovereign over the universe and everything in it, including world events, nature, and everything that touches your life. Here's the point: no matter what you may be waiting for, no matter who or what is blocking your progress or keeping you stuck, it is ultimately God you are waiting upon. To consider this another way, if you're "on hold" waiting for something, *pay attention* because God is at work in your life. Your waiting season is not happenstance; it's part of how God is growing you or changing something about you or your circumstances. But that doesn't mean you'll enjoy being in the waiting room! If there is one area of life that we chafe under and

> If you're "on hold" waiting for something, pay attention because God is at work in your life.

rebel against, it is waiting. We don't want to wait, but God clearly *does* want us to wait. How do we really know that? All we have to do is look thoughtfully at the natural world around us.

Nature Waits.

God has woven a time of waiting into nearly every aspect of the natural world. A garden is one example. After you plant seeds in the ground, no matter how excited you are to see the rewards of your work, you won't be harvesting anything the next day or even in the next few weeks. On the surface, for a long time it looks like your garden is a failure. You wait and wait but nothing is happening. But something actually is happening! Below the ground, where you cannot see it, nature is unfolding just the way it is supposed to. The seed coats are splitting open, moisture is causing the seeds to germinate, and they are beginning to grow. And then one day, green shoots pop through the earth! The seeds you planted are slowly turning into the vegetables or beautiful flowers you waited so long to see. And you realize that the time you spent waiting wasn't wasted; it was necessary.

Beyond the garden, the earth itself makes us wait. If you missed your chance to relax on the beach during the first low tide today, you'll have to coordinate your schedule with the ocean and try again later. If you missed today's sunrise or sunset, you'll have to wait a day to see the next one. If your busy schedule kept you from hiking amidst the autumn leaves this year, you'll have to put it on your calendar for next year.

Waiting is also part of the natural unfolding of human life. When a woman discovers that she is pregnant, no matter how excited she is to meet her baby, no fully developed baby will be in her arms the next day. Instead, she'll have to wait months until the birth day. For all of us, there's a long wait before we reach our full maturity. It takes years to grow from embryo to newborn to child to mature adult. Even after we're old enough to enter the work force, parts of our bodies are still maturing. The human brain, for example, is not fully mature until a person is in their mid to late twenties. Our bones don't reach their peak mass until we're twenty-five to thirty years old. Emotional maturity and spiritual growth take time as well. And so does learning. It takes time to learn to read and do math. It takes time, and sometimes years of practice, to perfect our skills and develop our natural talents.

Like the world around us, the micro-world within our bodies proceeds as if on a timer: the circadian rhythms that govern our sleeping and waking; ovulation; respiration; the beating of our hearts. We grow and develop and live our whole lives according to the mysterious inner biological clock God has placed within each of us.

We Are Bound by Time.

Waiting is an inevitable fact of life because, like all of nature, we are constrained to operate within the boundaries of time. By God's design, time literally forces us into periods of waiting. The most famous Bible passage about time is found in Ecclesiastes. You may know it as the lyrics to "Turn, Turn, Turn," a 1965 song by The Byrds. Except for the title, which repeats, and the last two lines of the song, the lyrics closely mirror Ecclesiastes 3.

There is a time for everything,
    and a season for every activity under the heavens:

    a time to be born and a time to die,
    a time to plant and a time to uproot,
    a time to kill and a time to heal,
    a time to tear down and a time to build,
    a time to weep and a time to laugh,
    a time to mourn and a time to dance,
    a time to scatter stones and a time to
        gather them,
    a time to embrace and a time to refrain
        from embracing,
    a time to search and a time to give up,
    a time to keep and a time to throw away,
    a time to tear and a time to mend,
    a time to be silent and a time to speak,
    a time to love and a time to hate,
    a time for war and a time for peace.

ECCLESIASTES 3:1-8

The Right Time

Ecclesiastes teaches us that waiting is not only woven into the rhythms of the natural world, but into the practical daily human experience as well: for everything there is a season, a time for every activity under heaven. There is a right time for everything, and this truth is further supported in both the Old and New Testaments:

- Jesus came at exactly the right time. "But when the *right time* came, God sent his Son, born of a woman, subject to the law" (Galatians 4:4 NLT).

- Jesus will return at exactly the right time. "And this is the plan: At the *right time* he will bring everything together under the authority of Christ—everything in heaven and on earth" (Ephesians 1:10 NLT).

- If we humble ourselves, God will honor us at the right time. "So humble yourselves under the mighty power of God, and at the *right time* he will lift you up in honor" (1 Peter 5:6 NLT).

- The right time to accept Christ as Savior is always today. "The *right time* is now. Today is the day of salvation" (2 Corinthians 6:2 NLT).

- There is a right time to awaken love. "Promise me, O women of Jerusalem, by the gazelles and wild deer, not to awaken love until the *right time*" (Song of Songs 2:7 NLT).

Since there was a right time for Jesus to be born, a right time for him to return, a right time for God to lift up the humble, and even a right time to awaken love, doesn't it make sense that there is also a "right time" for every event and next step of our lives? Jesus said that a sparrow doesn't fall from a tree apart from the knowledge of God (Matthew 10:29). He said that the hairs on our heads are numbered (Luke 12:7). That tiny detail, a fact we don't even know about ourselves, shows that God is aware of and concerned with the most intricate details of our lives as well as our big

---

Did you know that the New Testament, which was originally written in Greek, has two words for "time"? Both words, *chronos* and *kairos*, mean "time," but *kairos* time is different. It doesn't mean time in the sense of "It's four o'clock," but rather it is used to mean that something is done at the appropriate time or the appointed time for an occasion or event. When you read "the right time" in your Bible, most often it refers to *kairos* kind of time.

and little problems. Yet, when God wisely pushes the pause button to pace us so that things happen for us at the right time, we so often misunderstand, resist, and forge ahead. It's hard for us to accept that anything that slows us down could actually be positioning us to receive a blessing, right on time.

God Is Not in a Hurry.

God, the creator of time, is not subject to time. He exists outside of time, but we do not. We are bound by time, and for us, waiting has everything to do with time. The difficulty for us is when our timing (usually *now!*) does not sync with God's desire for us to sometimes wait. When we are boxed in by a circumstance we cannot change, waiting does not sit well with us. Not at all. We want things to happen at microwave speed and God seems to be on Crockpot™ time. Thus, one inescapable fact about waiting is that while we are in a hurry, God is not.

Throughout human history, God has always asked his people to wait:

- When God was ready to give Moses the Ten Commandments, he said, "Come up to me on the mountain and *wait there*" (Exodus 24:12 ESV).

- God chose David to be king when he was probably about fifteen years old, but his reign did not begin until he was thirty years old (2 Samuel 5:4).

- Simeon waited to see the Christ child because the Holy Spirit had revealed to him that he would not die until he had seen the Messiah (Luke 2:25–26).

- After Jesus had risen, he wanted his followers to know that God would send the Holy Spirit after he returned to heaven. He told them, "Do not leave Jerusalem, but *wait* for the gift my Father promised" (Acts 1:4).

- Around the world, believers are now waiting for the return of Christ (Hebrews 9:28).

On the pages of the Bible, we read about two categories of people who waited on God. Some waited for God to fulfill a specific promise he had made to them. Others had no special promise from God, but waited for something they deeply desired and prayed that God would grant.

Those Who Waited with a Promise

Throughout the ages, God has chosen certain people for special purposes and given them a promise that would fulfill the purpose he had called them to. Here are two examples of promises God made and kept by miraculously overriding the norms of nature.

Abraham and Sarah

- **The Promise Given**
  "'I will bless [Sarah] and will surely give you a son by her. I will bless her so that she will be the mother of nations; kings of peoples will come from her.' Abraham fell face down; he laughed and said to himself, 'Will a son be born to a man a hundred years old? Will Sarah bear a child at the age of ninety?'" (Genesis 17:16–17).

- **The Promise Fulfilled**
  "Sarah became pregnant and bore a son to Abraham in his old age, at the very time God had promised him" (Genesis 21:2).

Mary

- **The Promise Given**
  Old Testament: "The Lord himself will give you a sign: The virgin will conceive and give birth to a son, and will call him Immanuel" (Isaiah 7:14).

  New Testament: "The angel said to her, 'Do not be afraid, Mary; you have found favor with God. You will conceive and give birth to a son, and you are to call him Jesus. He will be great and will be called the Son of the Most High'" (Luke 1:30–32).

- **The Promise Fulfilled**
  "She gave birth to her firstborn, a son. She wrapped him in cloths and placed him in a manger" (Luke 2:7).

In a difference sense, all believers today are in the "waiting on a promise" category too because, as 1 John 2:25 says, "This is what he promised us—eternal life."

Those Who Waited without a Promise

God's people have always waited before him with the deep burdens of their hearts, telling him their needs and desires and interceding for others as well. The Bible mentions many by name. Hannah desperately wanted to have a child. Daniel fervently interceded for Jerusalem. Esther fasted to save the Jewish race from annihilation. Job prayed for his friends even as he was suffering. Solomon asked for a discerning heart.

Believers today are in this second category too. We bring our heartfelt requests to God and wait upon him to meet our needs and direct our steps. We ask him to guide us to the right job, to the right person to marry, and to the church where he would have us learn and serve. We pray for ourselves, our families and friends, and those who are seriously ill or in need of surgery. We pray for those going through divorce, or addicted to drugs, or in trouble with the law. We pray for our government and for those reeling from the impact of floods or fires or hurricanes. We cry out to God in our own emergencies, when car trouble has left us stranded alongside the road in the dark of night or when insurance won't cover our huge, unexpected medical bill.

Joseph was a lot like us in that, as far as we know, he had no specific promise from God. He waited for years, enduring much adversity, without knowing why he was suffering unjustly or what lay ahead for him. All the while, God was using his troubles to humble him, mature him, and prepare him for something bigger than he could ever have imagined. Though he was a Hebrew slave, wrongly imprisoned, God literally freed him from prison to become second in command in Egypt and save the world from famine.

Like Joseph, as we wait on God we may not know what we're really waiting for, or what God may be preparing us for. We're waiting for God to write the rest of our story! Many of the seeds that have been planted in our lives are still underground and we don't know yet when or what the harvest will be.

READ JOSEPH'S STORY

Joseph's story shows God's faithfulness while we wait—even if we don't understand why we're "on hold." The story begins in Genesis 37, resumes in chapter 39, and continues through chapter 41, where we find out what God was preparing Joseph for.

What parts of Joseph's story do you relate to most?

How is your story like Joseph's story? How is it different?

As Joseph's story continues to unfold in the chapters that follow, it gets even more amazing! Can you trust God with the parts of your story that have yet to unfold?

Waiting Is Proof of Trust.

Imagine that you are a member of a symphony orchestra being conducted by the composer of the music you are about to play. This amazing maestro is a master of every instrument in the orchestra and knows every sound that every instrument can produce. He is also personally acquainted with every member of the orchestra. He knows the extent of each musician's talent and the extent of their training. As he stands before the orchestra, recalling the entire musical score in precise detail, this virtuoso conducts with astonishing, unrivaled perfection.

Each orchestra member's job is to keep their eyes on the maestro and to play their part as he directs. They must play according to, and never apart from, the conductor's cues. Failing to do so would spoil the beauty of the music. So each musician gives their full attention to the maestro. They trust that because he composed the music himself, and because he has mastered every instrument, and because he is fully acquainted with every musician who sits before him, he can be trusted completely and followed precisely.

In human terms, God is like this symphony conductor. We are the individual members of the orchestra, fully known by God, who not only created the music our lives are to play, but also created each of us to play a specific part. When we play our notes too soon—when we run ahead of God—we spoil the music. When we play our notes too late, or refuse to play them at all, we likewise spoil the music. And when we have a "better idea" and break out into our own solo performance, we again spoil the music—the beautiful plan that God had in mind for us. As members of God's great, real-life orchestra of believers, our job is to keep our eyes on our Conductor, watching for our cues, trusting that his timing in our lives is actually truly perfect.

> "When we wait for him, we show that we trust him."
> CHARLES STANLEY

The more well-acquainted we are with the Word of God, the more we understand that our Conductor—God—is good. He is, in fact, the "goodest" good in the universe. All that he does is good; he can *only do* what is good. The more convinced we are of God's absolute goodness, the more we know that we can absolutely trust him. In Psalm 40:1 David tells us that he "waited patiently for the Lord." Charles Stanley, commenting on this verse, said, "When we wait for him, we show that we trust him."[1] God is indeed pleased when we trust in his goodness enough to wait on him. He responds by expressing that goodness all the more to us: *The Lord is good to those who wait for him, to the soul who seeks him.*

God Waits for Us.

Turn your attention for a moment to Isaiah 30:18 and notice who is doing the waiting, and why: "Therefore the Lord waits to be gracious to you, and therefore he exalts himself to show mercy to you" (esv). How amazing it is to know that God waits for us too! The God of the universe waits for you and me. And for what reason? So that he can show us grace and mercy.

In his 1896 devotional book, *Waiting on God*, Andrew Murray wrote:

> We must not only think of our waiting upon God, but also of what is more wonderful still, of God's waiting upon us. The vision of Him waiting on us ... will give us an unspeakable confidence that our waiting cannot be in vain. If He waits for us, then we may be sure that we are more than welcome; that He rejoices to find *those He has been seeking for....* He waits with all the longings of a father's heart. He waits that He may be gracious unto you. And each time you come to wait upon Him, or seek to maintain in daily life the holy habit of waiting, you may look up and see Him ready to meet you, waiting that He may be gracious unto you.[2]

God longs to connect with us! And he wants us to long for connection with him as well. But God, who knows human nature so well, knows that we resist connection with him until we have discovered that we can't unknot our lives apart from him. So he waits patiently for us until we become willing to wait for Him. It is blessed, wrote Murray, "when a waiting soul and a waiting God meet each other."[3]

The Heart

Connecting with God is unique in that, unlike our relationships with people, it is possible to sustain a continuous connection with him. This truest sense of waiting on God is evidence of a love relationship between the heavenly Father and his earthly child. When we live our lives close to God, we are more sensitive to the difference between seeking God's hand (what he can do for us) and seeking his face (who he is). We, like all of creation, wait on God for provision. While we must seek the hand of God, that is, his tangible help, our friendship with him has mostly to do with the heart. It is the heart, far more than the intellect, that seeks to know the person and personality of God. In Psalm 27:8, David expressed this idea so well: "My heart has heard you say, 'Come and talk with me.' And my heart responds, 'Lord, I am coming'" (NLT).

Andrew Murray wrote:

> All our waiting depends upon the state of the heart. As a man's heart is, so is he before God.... It is with the heart I must wait upon God; it is into the heart I must receive God.... Give your whole heart, with its secret workings, into God's hands continually.... In every true prayer there are two

hearts in exercise. The one is your heart, with its little, dark human thoughts of what you need and God can do. The other is God's great heart, with its infinite, its divine purposes of blessing.[4]

Our greatest challenge as believers is to fully wait upon and trust God's great heart. How sad and how unreasonable it is that instead of waiting on the sovereign authority, the "goodest" good, and the greatest love in the universe, we prefer to trust ourselves. Our power to make something happen or keep it from happening is nothing compared to his; we have zero knowledge of the future. And yet, we default to trusting our own limited knowledge, limited power, and limited wisdom, instead of waiting for God's great heart to guide us. When we look at it this way, we see that trusting ourselves rather than waiting on God doesn't actually make sense.

One reason we don't wait on and trust in God as fully as we could is because we don't know God as fully as we could. (Happily, there's a fix for that!)

Another reason we don't fully wait on him may have something to do with our particular personality. We can learn something about that from two of Jesus's closest followers.

Personality and Waiting on God

Some of us are more prone to run ahead of God than to wait on him. The go-getters among us, the "let's get this done" people who run fast and hard in business and in life, may find it most difficult to wait on God. Those who are naturally laid back and reflective when deciding about most everything may find it much easier to wait on God to resolve a problem, open a door of opportunity, or provide guidance through his Word.

It's good for each of us to recognize whether our natural tendency is to forge ahead or to hold back. One personality type isn't better than the other; God created both. And Jesus picked people with both personality types to be his closest followers. Consider how different Peter and Thomas were.

Throughout the gospels we see Peter saying and doing things that reveal his impulsive, "let's do this!" personality. He was the one who boldly got out of the boat to walk on water. He was the one who dared to reprimand Jesus when he revealed that his death and resurrection lay ahead. Peter was the one who impulsively promised the Lord, "Even if everyone else deserts you, I will never desert you," and of course, that very night Peter denied him three times. Earlier that same night, when the mob showed up to take Jesus away, it was Peter who impulsively drew his sword and cut off the ear of Malchus, the high priest's servant.

> The more convinced we are of God's absolute goodness, the more we know that we can absolutely trust him.

Thomas, a.k.a. "doubting Thomas," had the opposite personality type. He was the last disciple to believe that Jesus had really been raised from the dead. The others told him, "We have seen the Lord!" But he said to them, "Unless I see the nail marks in his hands and put my finger where the nails were, and put my hand into his side, I will not believe" (John 20:25).

An Old Testament example of the more cautious personality type is Gideon. He wanted to be really sure about what God was asking him to do, so he asked God to prove it by giving him a sign. He told God, "I will put a wool fleece on the threshing floor tonight. If the fleece is wet with dew in the morning but the ground is dry, then I will know that you are going to help me rescue Israel as you promised." The Bible reports that God gave him the sign he asked for and "the next morning, he squeezed the fleece and wrung out a whole bowlful of water" (Judges 6:37–38 NLT). But Gideon wanted to be really, *really* sure, so he asked for another sign, which God also graciously granted.

Here's the point. While Peter had a personality that made him prone to leap ahead without much thought, Thomas and Gideon had personalities that made them cautious and skeptical. Though they had opposite temperaments, God loved them all and used them all to accomplish his purposes.

What's interesting is that after Jesus was raised from the dead and had returned to heaven, and the Holy Spirit came to dwell in believers, Peter was dramatically changed. Now filled with the Spirit, Peter matured spiritually. As his outgoing personality was tempered with wisdom and restraint, he became a great leader. Peter counseled the early church, and us as well through the Word, to adopt and imitate his mature and balanced approach:

> *Prepare your minds for action
> and exercise self-control.*
>
> 1 PETER 1:13 NLT

No doubt speaking from past experience, Peter encourages us to let self-control govern our desires so we don't act too quickly.

PERSONALITY AND WAITING: THREE THINGS TO THINK ABOUT

1. **Which best describes your personality?**

   ❑ "Let's go for it" like Peter

   ❑ "Let's be sure about this" like Thomas and Gideon

   ❑ A blend of both, or it depends on the situation

2. **Which do you tend to do more often?**

   ❑ Impulsively leap forward when it may be more prudent to wait

   ❑ Linger with an over-abundance of caution when it may be time to step out on faith

3. **Peter told the early church to do two things: "Prepare your minds for action and exercise self-control." Which is easier for you to do?**

   ❑ Prepare your mind for action

   ❑ Exercise self-control

As you continue reading, think about how your personality may influence your waiting on God.

Chapter 2
If You're Waiting, God Is Working

THE BIBLE DESCRIBES SEVERAL OCCASIONS WHEN God caused something to happen immediately. One of those times was when Ananias was sent to Saul (later called Paul), who had been blind for three days. He placed his hands on Saul and told him why he had come. The Bible reports, "*Immediately*, something like scales fell from Saul's eyes, and he could see again" (Acts 9:18).

Another time, a woman who had been bleeding for twelve years came up behind Jesus in a crowd and touched his cloak, thinking, "If I just touch his clothes,

I will be healed." The Bible tells us, "*Immediately* her bleeding stopped, and she felt in her body that she was freed from her suffering" (Mark 5:29).

In yet another story, Paul and Silas were in prison, praying and singing hymns around midnight. "Suddenly, there was a massive earthquake, and the prison was shaken to its foundations. All the doors *immediately* flew open, and the chains of every prisoner fell off!" (Acts 16:26 NLT).

In the modern era, though we must often wait for answers to our prayers, sometimes we're surprised by how swiftly God responds. The classic devotional book *Streams in the Desert* includes a story about George Mueller, a nineteenth-century minister and philanthropist who often experienced amazing answers to his prayers. The story was told by a steam ship captain who, due to adverse weather, had been on the bridge of the ship for twenty-four hours:

> George Mueller came to me, and said, "Captain I have come to tell you that I must be in Quebec Saturday afternoon." "It is impossible," I said. "Very well, if your ship cannot take me, God will find some other way. I have never broken an engagement for fifty-seven years. Let us go down into the chart-room and pray."

I looked at that man of God, and thought to myself, what lunatic asylum can that man have come from? I never heard of such a thing as this. "Mr. Mueller," I said, "do you know how dense this fog is?" "No," he replied, "my eye is not on the density of the fog, but on the living God, who controls every circumstance of my life."

He knelt down and prayed one of the most simple prayers, and when he had finished I was going to pray; but he put his hand on my shoulder, and told me not to pray. "First, you do not believe He will answer; and second I BELIEVE HE HAS, and there is no need whatever for you to pray about it."

I looked at him, and he said, "Captain, I have known my Lord for fifty-seven years, and there has never been a single day that I have failed to get audience with the King. Get up, Captain and open the door, and you will find the fog gone." I got up, and the fog was indeed gone. On Saturday afternoon, George Mueller was in Quebec for his engagement.[5]

> "For since the world began, no ear has heard
> and no eye has seen a God like you,
> who works for those who wait for him!"
>
> ISAIAH 64:4 NLT

When God Says Wait

Why does our sovereign God, who loves us dearly—and could instantly answer our every prayer—rarely act as immediately for us as he did in the stories above? Why does he so often instead make us wait?

To even begin exploring the answers to these questions, it is vital to first understand that though waiting can be frustrating, disappointing, and irritating, God is not playing with our lives. He doesn't make us wait just because he can. Lamentations 3:33 assures us that God "takes no pleasure in ... throwing roadblocks in the way" (MSG, paraphrase). In other words, whenever God makes us wait, there is a purpose for it. While we may not always know what that purpose is, the story of Lazarus in John 11:1–43 reveals how waiting can be essential to God's plan.

When Jesus received word that his good friend Lazarus had died, instead of immediately going to comfort

Lazarus's sisters, his friends Mary and Martha, he waited for two days right where he was. When he finally arrived in Bethany, the town where his friends lived, Lazarus had already been in the tomb for four days. Martha went out to meet Jesus and told him, "Lord, if you had been here, my brother would not have died." Jesus responded, "Your brother will rise again." Martha said, "I know he will rise again in the resurrection at the last day." Jesus then said something to her that hinted at why he had come: "I am the resurrection and the life. The one who believes in me will live, even though they die; and whoever lives by believing in me will never die."

When Mary joined them, she fell at Jesus's feet weeping. The Bible's account of this moment says, "When Jesus saw her weeping, and the Jews who had come along with her also weeping, he was deeply moved in spirit and troubled." And then Jesus wept too.

At the tomb, Jesus said, "Take away the stone." Martha cautioned, "But, Lord, by this time there is a bad odor, for he has been there four days." Jesus told her, "Did I not tell you that if you believe, you will see the glory of God?" So they took away the stone. Then Jesus looked up and said, "Father, I thank you that you have heard me. I knew that you always hear me, but I said this for the benefit of the people standing here, that they may believe that you sent me."

When he had said this, Jesus called in a loud voice, "Lazarus, come out!" The dead man came out, his hands and feet wrapped with strips of linen, and a cloth around his face. Jesus said to them, "Take off the grave clothes and let him go."

It was an astonishing miracle! But why didn't Jesus do it sooner? Why, knowing that Mary, Martha, and many others were grieving, did he wait so long? Jesus had deliberately arrived in Bethany exactly when he planned to: when Lazarus had been in the tomb for four days. But why? BibleRef.com explains:

> The long delay was not an accident. Modern medicine allows very precise measurement of heart and brain function. In the ancient world, it was not impossible for a person to seem dead, but recover. For that reason, death was often not considered "official" until a few days later. Jesus' three days and nights in the tomb corresponds to this custom. In Lazarus' case, many Jewish people considered the fourth day to be when the soul was considered truly gone.... In other words, Jesus has purposefully set up this scenario. The moment was not an accident, but an arrangement.[6]

Jesus knew that people commonly believed that a soul lingered for three days after death. He knew that on the fourth day, everyone who was gathered at the tomb would consider Lazarus to be truly dead and his spirit now gone from earth. By raising Lazarus from the dead on the fourth day, Jesus was clearly proclaiming himself to be God, who alone has power over death. The Jamieson-Fausset-Brown commentary affirms that this was the claim Jesus was making. In light of Jesus's words to Martha—"I am the resurrection and the life"—the authors say, "What higher claim to supreme divinity than this grand saying can be conceived?"[7] Because Jesus waited until just the right time to perform this miracle, it resulted in undeniable proof of his deity.

Why God May Make You Wait

Whenever we encounter circumstances we cannot change or when we can't make something happen on our timetable, it's normal to wonder why we are on hold, reluctantly stuck in the waiting room. Since God's thoughts and plans are so much higher than ours, we may not always be able to answer the why question. Sometimes, however, we can discern the reason. Here are six possible reasons why God may make you wait.

1. God may be answering your prayers.

Whenever you're waiting for something, the first thing to consider is that God may be answering your prayers! That is, while you're waiting, God may be aligning the very circumstances that will become the answer to your prayer. While he does sometimes work in a miraculous way, most of the time he works within the normal time constraints and physical boundaries that govern our world and our lives. Sometimes, things must unfold in a certain natural sequence, and God may simply be allowing that to happen. Waiting may just be a practical necessity: someone else may need to change their mind about something, or a series of events may need to fall like dominoes before you see the answer to your prayer.

2. It may be preparation for something new.

When the seasons of life are changing, waiting can be a time of reflection and inward preparation for what lies ahead. Whether it's a new job, a new relationship, a new sense of direction, a new city, or a new solution to an old problem, God is never just concerned with our circumstances. He's always more concerned with what's going on inside of us, the things that define our character, such as our integrity, motives, and thought life. So while you wait for what's next, let God prepare your heart as well as your circumstances.

A pause before a new chapter of life is actually quite biblical. Frances Ridley Havergal, a nineteenth-century English hymn writer, once observed, "Did you ever hear of anyone being much used of Christ who did not have some special waiting time?"[8] She was right. Even the apostle Paul needed a three-year waiting season before he could embrace God's unique call on his life (Galatians 1:15–18).

3. It may be a test of faith.

The Bible tells us in several places that God sometimes tests us:

- In Genesis, we read, "God tested Abraham" (Genesis 22:1).

- In Exodus, Moses told the people, "God has come to test you" (Exodus 20:20).

- In the book of Jeremiah, the prophet spoke to God saying, "You test those who are righteous" (Jeremiah 20:12 NLT).

- In Psalms, David wrote, "The Lord tests the righteous" (Psalm 11:5 ESV).

When God doesn't respond quickly to our prayers, forcing us to wait on him, it tests us, not to defeat or discourage us, but quite the opposite. When there is a long time lag between our praying and God's answering, it may be so that we will wrestle with our doubts and overcome them with a deeper trust that enables us to go on waiting. Sometimes doubts may flourish during a time of waiting because, as you may have heard it said, "The teacher is always quiet during the test."

If you are finding it hard to endure the test of waiting, James has some encouragement for you: "The testing of your faith produces perseverance. Let perseverance finish its work so that you may be mature and complete, not lacking anything" (James 1:3–4).

4. It may be a wake-up call about control.

When things are going well for us, we feel like we're in control. Everything is going our way because we're doing such a great job, right? We've got this! Until we are sidelined by a circumstance that forces us to wait, we don't realize that control is just an illusion. But when we hit

> Waiting forces us to release our white-knuckle grip on the illusion of control.

a wall and we cannot change our circumstances no matter how hard we try, how much we cry, or how fervently we pray, we have to face the fact that we are not in control. Waiting reveals our powerlessness. It forces us to release our white-knuckle grip on the illusion of control. It teaches us the truth: we are not in control; God is.

5. It may not be the right time.

As noted in the last chapter, there is a right time for everything. But we often forget that our timetable may not be the same as God's timetable. While we may want an answer now, we may not be ready for it yet. Andrew Murray spoke to the frustration of this in his classic devotional book. Having just mentioned that God waits for us to seek him so that he can be gracious to us, he continued:

How is it, if He waits to be gracious, that even after I come and wait upon Him, He does not give the help I seek, but waits on longer and longer?... God is a wise [farmer], who "waiteth for the precious fruit of the earth, and hath long patience for it"[James 5:7]. He cannot gather the fruit till it is ripe. He knows when we are spiritually ready to receive the blessing to our profit and His glory.... Be assured that if God waits longer than you could wish, it is only to make the blessing doubly precious. God waited four thousand years, till the fullness of time, ere He sent His Son: our times are in His hands [Psalm 31:15].... He will make haste for our help, and not delay one hour too long.[9]

6. It may be about your relationship with God.

It's been said that when God doesn't have your attention, he'll disturb what does. One way he can reclaim our attention is by pushing the pause button on something we cherish more than we cherish him. Anything we cherish more than God is, in biblical terms, an idol. When God decreed, "You shall have no other gods before me" (Exodus 20:3), he was not just making a suggestion! The experience of waiting can be a humbling reminder that God wants and deserves first place in our lives.

Andrew Murray believed this. He wrote:

> At our first entrance into the school of waiting upon God, the heart is chiefly set upon the blessings which we wait for. God graciously uses our need and desire for help to educate us for something higher than we were thinking of. We were seeking gifts; He, the Giver, longs to give Himself and to satisfy the soul with His goodness. It is just for this reason that He often withholds the gifts, and that the time of waiting is made so long. He is all the time seeking to win the heart of His child for Himself.[10]

JOURNAL EXERCISE

Sometimes with thoughtful, prayerful reflection, we may be able to discern the reason we're in "the waiting room."

Set aside some quiet time alone to re-read and reflect upon each section under the "Why God May Make You Wait" heading. Then, with paper and pen in hand (or on your computer or in the space provided below), journal your thoughts and questions, asking the Lord to give you insight and direction for your unique circumstances.

1. God may be answering your prayers.

2. It may be preparation for something new.

3. It may be a test of faith.

4. It may be a wake-up call about control.

5. It may not be the right time.

6. It may be about your relationship with God.

How Should We Wait on God?

As this chapter's title says, if you're waiting, God is working—but he's not just working in your *circumstances*. Whether you see your situation changing yet or not, God can and does use waiting to change you. In fact, as Pastor T. D. Jakes has said, "The thing that is the most important to God are the things that happen to you while you're waiting."[11] That's why when waiting is all you can do, it's the best thing you can do. Waiting on God is never a waste of time. As long as we're still waiting, God is still working, and always for our good.

Even in times of "happy waiting"—anticipating the birth of a baby or counting the days till Christmas, for example—no one ever wants to wait longer than necessary! Can *how* we wait play a role in *how long* we wait? Pastor Jakes's insights seem to suggest that the answer is yes.

How then should we wait before God? Here are five suggestions.

1. Wait patiently.

> "Love is patient."
> 1 CORINTHIANS 13:4

In 1 Corinthians 13, it is interesting to note that *patient* is the first word Paul uses to describe love. Patience is also a fruit of the Spirit (Galatians 5:22), which means that the Holy Spirit, not us, grows our patience as we struggle to wait. Because God is himself the ultimate expression of both love and patience, when it is his will for us to *keep on waiting*, we can persevere, drawing upon his infinite patience to help us. And that's a very good thing because when waiting goes on and on and on, a more durable, more mature form of patience is needed.

This deeper patience, called *longsuffering*, is, in fact, a form of suffering. When waiting turns into longsuffering, although it's more difficult to endure, it can create a deeper intimacy with Christ than would otherwise be possible. Under the weight of longsuffering, the roots of both patience and faith, as if seeking for water, go deeper and deeper in search of God, and a special relationship develops. Those who wait before God from this more deeply rooted place are like the orchestra members in the first chapter, keeping their eyes firmly fixed on the symphony conductor. They are learning to trust him more completely and follow him more precisely because longsuffering has given them a glimpse of how extraordinary he really is.

2. Wait expectantly.

> "I lay my requests before you
> and wait expectantly."
>
> PSALM 5:3

The Merriam-Webster thesaurus offers many synonyms for the word *expectantly*. Some of them are *lightheartedly*, *joyously*, *exuberantly*, *positively*, *cheerily*, and *giddily*. There's excitement and energy in those words! Think of toddlers jumping up and down at the front door because daddy's car just pulled into the driveway. Think of your dog turning circles in the kitchen as soon as you start to fill her supper dish. The kids and Scruffy are *waiting expectantly*, bursting with delight and anticipation.

Though we may not experience the same intensity of emotion when we wait expectantly before the Lord, grown-up hearts do still stir with anticipation and excitement. We can wait expectantly, even joyfully, on God because we know he has heard the requests we have laid before him and because we know he delights in us.

Hearts that are desperate also wait expectantly on God. The psalmist wrote, "I wait for the LORD more than watchmen wait for the morning" (Psalm 130:6). And why did night watchmen so yearn for daybreak in those ancient times? It was because of the terrors watchmen encountered at night. Tempests at sea. Shipwrecked vessels. Drowning men. On land, armies taken by surprise in the dark of night, now surrounded by the enemy. No wonder watchmen waited desperately for the dawn. The sunrise brought light. Light reveals the enemy's location. Light brings a chance for a better rescue at sea. Light brings hope. The psalmist picked this metaphor to show what it means to wait *expectantly* on God. And he said he waits for God even more expectantly than night watchmen wait for the sunrise.

3. Wait prayerfully.

> "Pray continually."
> 1 THESSALONIANS 5:17

Whether uttered silently in the heart or spoken aloud, the Bible assures us that fervent prayer has great power and accomplishes much (James 5:16). Thus, prayer is not passive; it is spiritual work. And because we are to present our requests to God "in every situation" (Philippians 4:6), there is no circumstance too small or too hopeless to bring to God in prayer.

When we wait before God in prayer, it does not matter how eloquently or poorly we express ourselves with words because God always hears our hearts. We are to pray "on all occasions" (Ephesians 6:18)—on quiet, ordinary days when not much seems to be happening, and on days when we are overwhelmed or stressed-out because *too much* is happening. We need God's continual protection, direction, and wisdom, not just when we're facing a crisis or making pivotal life decisions, but in our most mundane everyday decisions as well.

Sometimes we pray with urgency because it's time for us to take action. We need God to intervene in our circumstances—not so we don't have to make hard decisions, but because we need courage and wisdom to make the *right* decisions. Sometimes we pray with urgency because we cannot take any action. When we are powerless and can only wait, it's a comfort to know that God is present in all the places we cannot go: the womb where a baby is mysteriously being formed, or the surgical suite where a loved one lies on an operating table.

Be assured of this: whenever you meet a situation or circumstance head-on in prayer, spiritually speaking, you have taken the ultimate action step.

4. Wait confidently.

> "My heart is confident in you, O God;
> my heart is confident."
> PSALM 57:7 NLT

David, who wrote Psalm 57, waited before God with confidence, knowing his prayers were heard. As a shepherd himself, David was able to say with confidence, "The Lord is my shepherd, I lack nothing" (Psalm 23:1). The more we understand about the character and infinite capabilities of God, the more confident we too can be in all our waiting and praying and living before him.

5. Wait hopefully.

> "If we hope for what we do not yet have,
> we wait for it patiently."
>
> ROMANS 8:25

Waiting implies that change is possible. So almost by definition, waiting involves hope. And until a delay becomes a denial, there is always room for hope! Hope is a catalyst. It's what compels us to persevere in prayer and to wait patiently for the things we do not yet have. When we hope for something, we envision it; we deeply desire it, and we long for it to happen. When we wait before God, speaking to him of our most cherished hopes, it is because we know that apart from his help, we lack the power to make our hope a reality. Hope is our strong tether to God while we are in the waiting room.

HOW TO WAIT ON THE LORD

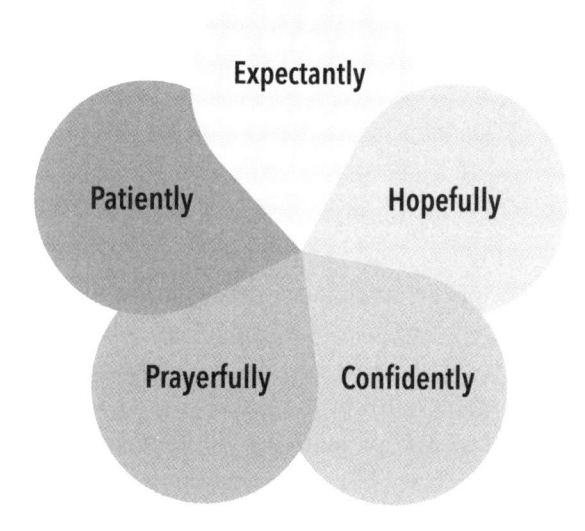

- Expectantly
- Patiently
- Hopefully
- Prayerfully
- Confidently

Which aspects of waiting on God do you think are most important for you?

Which do you find easy?

Which are most difficult for you?

A Wiser Way to Wait

A young woman named Katie was frustrated because, despite much praying, she had not yet met "the one," the man she would marry. When she voiced her frustration to a counselor, he responded with some questions about how and where she was spending her time. As Katie spoke about her lifestyle, it wasn't hard for the counselor to see why she hadn't met the love of her life. She worked during the day and spent most evenings at home by herself. She did occasionally go out with her girlfriends, and she went to church on Sunday. Seeing her pattern, the counselor easily identified the problem: she wasn't ever crossing paths with any young men she might date!

The counselor suggested that Katie add some activities and join some groups where she could meet more people. She took his advice. She had fun, met new people, and some men began to ask her out on dates. One of them was the man who eventually became her husband.

The wisdom behind the counselor's suggestion was based on the simple truth that God has ordered real life in such a way that people and circumstances respond to action. Prayer is the action step that prepares the way, but then we must also get out of our "prayer chair" and step out into the world, trusting that because God has heard our prayer, he will guide us. If Katie had continued to only pray and to stay home alone every evening, she probably would never have met the man she was to marry. She would have lived her whole life disappointed that God did not answer her prayer, not understanding that she had a role to play in God's answer.

That's how waiting on God usually works! We must pray and wait and then also be willing to take action in ways that correspond to how God has designed the world to work. But here's the extremely important thing: waiting on God is not "one size fits all." While Katie's story does demonstrate how God so often works, we must be sensitive to his guidance in our particular situation. One person may need to pray and wait a very long time before taking a step. Someone else may need to pray and then act quickly. Another person may need to take no action at all and just "stand still and see this great thing the Lord is about to do before your eyes!" (1 Samuel 12:16). Well-meaning, sincere Christians may be prayerful and wait patiently, but too passively,

> The key is to discern God's wisdom for your situation and act accordingly.

believing, as Katie first did, that they have no role to play in the outcome. At the other extreme are well-meaning, sincere Christians who wait prayerfully and patiently for a while, but then, because of fear or impatience, as if everything depended on them, they run ahead of God. The key is to discern God's wisdom for your situation and act accordingly. Here are some tips that may help you do that.

Remember who you're waiting for.

God has many names. Each one displays some facet of his character, wisdom, or amazing love. When we wait on him for specific things, we can speak to him using his special name that relates most to our need.

- One of God's names is Jehovah-Jirah, which means "the God who provides." If you are waiting before God because you need a job or wisdom or some kind of help, speak to Jehovah-Jirah about your need.

- Is your heart in turmoil? Reach out to Jehovah-Shalom, the God of peace.

- Are you in a battle with temptation? Jehovah-M'Kaddesh, the God who sanctifies, can strengthen your resistance and your resolve to do the right thing.

- Do you want to draw near to God as father? Abba means father or daddy.

- Do you need physical, moral, mental, or emotional healing? Let Jehovah-Rapha, the Lord our healer, guide you to find the help you need. He is the God of all Comfort who can comfort you in your season of waiting (2 Corinthians 1:3–4).

- He is also Jehovah-Raah, the Lord my shepherd; Immanuel, God with us, and El Deah, the God of knowledge.

God has dozens of names throughout the Bible! When we consider how specific and varied his many names are, we begin to comprehend his completeness and perfection. No matter what you are waiting for, your Father, comforter, healer, shepherd, and sanctifier, the all-knowing, always-present one, sees you, hears you, and knows you perfectly. This is the God you wait for. (See the resources at the end of this book to find a link to nearly one hundred names of God.)

Don't get mad at God.

Sometimes God says no.

If you have prayed and waited, and prayed and waited, only to be disappointed by a no, here's what you can be sure of: God is greater than the no. He is greater than any roadblock that led to the no. If the thing that did not open up to you is in fact the thing that God wants for you, if you persevere, the way forward will open up. But if the no won't budge, God may be using that closed door or mistake or misunderstanding to redirect your steps. It may be that the no was because God has a better, greater good in mind for you. We know that because God is pure goodness, the "goodest" good, he can only do good. So when he delays an answer, it is for our good. And the same is true when his answer is no.

The apostle Paul had a physical affliction which he described as a thorn in his flesh. He asked God, not once but three times, to remove it, yet God did not remove it. Paul knew why God said no. God had given him "surpassingly great revelations" and because of this, Paul said, "In order to keep me from becoming conceited, I was given a thorn in my flesh" (2 Corinthians 12:6–9). Unlike Paul, we don't always know the reason for our no or yes. What we do know, however, is as Dr. Charles Stanley once said, "If God is withholding an answer to your prayer, it is an act of pure, sovereign love."[12]

There are two ways to receive a disappointing no that we don't understand, and we have a choice about how we will respond. We can choose to respond with trust, believing that this no is a door to something better. The other choice is to respond with resentment toward God for not giving us what we wanted. In other words, we can be mad at God for closing the door we still want to go through, or we can see the no as redirection. Either way, when the answer is no, the question becomes, what's next? And we may find ourselves back in the waiting room again.

Keep calm and carry on.

In 1939, as World War II was looming as a threat to the United Kingdom, the government prepared three posters it hoped would raise public morale. One of the posters displayed the slogan KEEP CALM AND CARRY ON under an image of the Tudor Crown. The plan was to distribute the two other posters and retain the Keep Calm poster for later use. But because the first two posters were unpopular, the Keep Calm poster was never distributed. Many years later, the slogan soared to popularity after English bookstore owners found an original poster in a box of used books they bought at an auction in 2000.

Several years ago, an article about waiting on God posed the question, "When things aren't working out, when God seems silent, when life is at a standstill and every path seems like a wrong turn, what do we do?"[13] If that's the question you're asking, there's some good advice for you on an old British poster: KEEP CALM AND CARRY ON—because God's got you and he's got the master plan!

Four Ways to Keep Calm and Carry On

While you are waiting on God for direction—or redirection—here are four ideas that may help you to keep calm and carry on. As you read through them, you may want to journal your thoughts on paper, on your computer, or in the space provided, asking the Lord to give you insights and direction for your unique circumstances.

1. Acknowledge your emotions.

It bears repeating: waiting is hard. Even when we are certain that David's words in Psalm 138 are true— "The Lord will work out his plans for my life"— waiting is still hard. As we wait on God, David's plea at the end of the psalm may also resonate: "Don't abandon me, for you made me" (Psalm 138:8 NLT).

Waiting can make us feel alone, discouraged, frustrated, afraid, worried, and so many other emotions. Emotions are neither right nor wrong; they're just feelings. God created the entire spectrum of human emotions, so no matter what we're feeling, God understands. There's no need to deny our emotions. We can call them by name and acknowledge them and just talk to God about whatever we're feeling.

- What emotions has your time in "the waiting room" triggered? (Call them by name.)

- Which of those emotions are the most difficult for you to acknowledge? (Say them out loud.)

- Talk to God about the emotions you have acknowledged. If you are putting your thoughts in writing, you may prefer to share with God in a letter.

2. Align your life with the Word.

Andrew Murray again guides us with wisdom: "When waiting on God, we need to be very careful that we keep His ways; out of these we never can expect to find Him.... If we do not keep His ways, our waiting on Him can bring no blessing."[14]

With this counsel in mind, take a moment to introspect honestly. Pray this prayer from King David in Psalm 139:23–24: "Search me, God, and know my heart; test me and know my anxious thoughts. See if there is any offensive way in me, and lead me in the way everlasting."

- Is there anything in God's Word that you are choosing to disobey? Any "gray area" that might not look so gray in the bright light of the Scriptures?

- If there is something, take the opportunity to realign your life with God's Word as you wait before him. What needs to change in your life?

3. Focus on the present.

We can learn from the past and prepare as best we can for the future, but we can only wait on God in the present, one day at a time. While you wait, don't let regrets about the past or concerns about the future keep you from inviting God into all your present moments.

If you find yourself focusing more on the past or the future than the present, the "5-4-3-2-1 technique" may help. This simple exercise helps you use your five senses to call your attention back to the present. Here's how:

- Look around and name *5* things that you see.
- Listen until you can name *4* things that you hear.
- Touch *3* things around you, such as the chair you're sitting in.
- Breathe in through your nose and identify *2* things that you smell.
- Name *1* thing you taste, such as your water, gum, lip balm, or even the inside of your mouth.

4. Make the most of your waiting time.

In Exodus 4:2, the Lord asks Moses, "What is that in your hand?"

Moses says, "a staff."

There wasn't anything special about Moses's staff. As objects go, it was pretty ordinary. It was just a tool of the shepherd's trade, useful for rescuing sheep or fighting off wild beasts. It was made of wood and certainly not valuable in a monetary sense. And yet, when the staff was surrendered to God, amazing things happened. Moses used it to part the Red Sea and get water out of a rock.

- If God can use something as humble and ordinary as a shepherd's staff, he can surely use anything. Look closely—what's in *your* hand? Whatever it is, surrender it to God.

- While you wait, how can you make use of what God has seen fit to place in your hand? Don't just bide your time in the waiting room. Get creative, make the most of it, and see what happens!

Chapter 3
The Mystery of Waiting

JUST AS GOD ESTABLISHED THE INVISIBLE LAWS THAT govern the physical world—the law of gravity, the laws of physics, the rhythms of day and night and the ocean tides—he also set in motion unseen principles that govern our relationship with him. One of the most important principles is waiting on God. Because God's timing is always perfect, never too early and never too late, he wants us to allow his perfect timing to guide our lives. Thus, he wants us to wait for his timing in all things. This dependent connection with the unseen, omnipotent God of the universe is, to the human mind, a wondrous mystery.

God's Mysterious Ways

To know God's timing, we must wait for him to reveal it to us. If we're not really that interested in knowing God or his plan for us, he won't force it upon us. He will gladly reveal it, however, to anyone who is sincerely seeking him and his direction for their life. We'll be frustrated though if we expect him to respond on our timetable. He will answer us just as he does all other things: when the time is right.

Isaiah 55:8 tells us that God's thoughts and ways are nothing like ours; they are higher and wiser. We easily accept this as fact because, after all, he is God, right? But because his ways are so far beyond anything we can even imagine, they often don't make sense to us. And when those higher, wiser ways make us wait, we're often surprised, and maybe a little irritated too: what is he *doing*?

> "My thoughts are nothing like your thoughts," says the Lord. "And my ways are far beyond anything you could imagine."
>
> ISAIAH 55:8 NLT

We naturally expect God to respond in ways that seem rational and reasonable to us. While he does sometimes do that, other times, to our great consternation, he does not. What we forget is that God knows what we do not know. He knows what the future holds, and because his love for us is as perfect as his timing, he will always do what's best for us if it is different than what we have asked for. When his answers don't match our expectations, we're often perplexed. No wonder Paul wrote, "How impossible it is for us to understand his decisions and his ways!" (Romans 11:33 NLT).

We might be somewhat less perplexed by God's higher, wiser answers if we begin to expect him to respond in ways that surprise us.

Sometimes God answers in ways we could never have imagined.

For example, who would ever have thought that God would accomplish our salvation in the way he did? Jesus left the perfection of heaven and humbled himself to take on human flesh, entering the world as a helpless newborn baby. The circumstances were supernatural: he was conceived by the Holy Spirit in the womb of a virgin teenage girl. He grew up in submission to human parents. He walked the earth for only thirty-three years and died a horrible death by crucifixion to be the human sacrifice for the sins of the world.

If you or I had designed the plan of salvation, we would never have done it this way. This is why the song "A Strange Way to Save the World" resonates so deeply with many of us. (Find links to this amazing song in the resources in the back of this book.) We wait upon the very same God! Why should we be surprised if he chooses to answer our prayers in ways we could never have imagined?

Sometimes God answers so subtly that his handiwork may only be realized in hindsight.

Many of God's answers occur "as"—that is, *as* we are living life normally and *as* we are just doing what we know to do while waiting on God. "As" is how the miracle occurred in Matthew, chapter 15. There was a problem: too many people and a pitifully small amount of food to share. But *as* the disciples were distributing the seven loaves of bread and few small fish that Jesus had blessed, these meager resources multiplied to feed four thousand men and their families. The miraculous unfolded as the humblest of foods—bread and fish—were simply torn into pieces and given away. We serve the same God! He still delights in sometimes breaking in on our everyday lives in unexpected ways *as* we're just doing normal things while waiting for his answers. Sometimes we don't realize until we look back later that the Lord's fingerprints are all over the unexpected thing that happened and met our need.

Sometimes God answers at unexpected times.

As we read in Ecclesiastes, there is a "right time" for everything, and God alone is the sovereign scheduler of events. Our challenge is trusting that God will move in our personal circumstances at the right time and also bring about the answers to our prayers at the right time. God's timing is a mystery: sometimes God answers before the "amen" is even spoken, as with George Mueller on board the steam ship; other times, the answer comes months or years later when we least expect it.

The Mystery of Spiritual Growth

God has revealed part of his plan for each one of us: we are "predestined to be conformed to the image of his Son" (Romans 8:29). In other words, he is making us like Jesus, not outwardly, but inwardly. What's interesting is that the verse that comes right before this is the one we use to encourage each other when things are not going well or have become difficult to bear: "All things work together for good, for those who are called according to his purpose" (Romans 8:28 ESV). These verses go together because the disappointing and difficult events of our lives are part of how God shapes and molds us to be more like Jesus. Because waiting is difficult, it is also a part of the mysterious process of being made Christlike.

> Waiting is part of the mysterious process of being made Christlike.

Muscles grow when they are forced to endure the pressure of heavier and heavier weights. Spiritual growth works the same way. If we surrender the full weight of our frustration and disappointment to God when he sees fit to make us wait, we learn patience and self-control. While brief times of waiting can be inconvenient and irritating, as mentioned before, long periods of waiting can be a form of suffering. The more difficult the waiting situation, the more suffering it causes us and the more we must persevere. Psalm 119:81 could be the theme verse for those who are longsuffering: "I am worn out waiting for your rescue, but I have put my hope in your word" (NLT).

The suffering we endure while waiting can bring on a cascade of spiritual growth: "Suffering produces perseverance; perseverance, character; and character, hope" (Romans 5:3–4). Thus, waiting is one of God's favorite tools for making us more like Jesus. We can't help but wonder at the irony though: how is it that the weariness and difficulty of waiting can produce the exquisite and joyful fruits of Christlike character? That's the mystery of it.

The Mystery of Persistent Prayer

When we do not yet see the answer to a prayer, Jesus has told us what to do while we wait for it: "Keep on asking, and you will receive what you ask for. Keep on seeking, and you will find. Keep on knocking, and the door will be opened to you" (Luke 11:9 NLT). So we are to persist in prayer. But why? After all, the Bible tells us elsewhere that God knows what we need before we ask (Matthew 6:8).

As we have seen, there can be many reasons why God may want us to wait, and we often do not know what the reason is. There is one passage in the Bible that pulls back the curtain between us and the spiritual realm just enough to show us that there may sometimes be more to unanswered prayer than we can perceive.

> "Keep on asking, and you will receive what you ask for. Keep on seeking, and you will find. Keep on knocking, and the door will be opened to you."
>
> LUKE 11:9 NLT

Daniel had been fasting and praying for three weeks when he was given an amazing vision about what would take place far in the future. The appearance of the angel who brought the vision was so astonishing that Daniel's strength left him, his face grew deathly pale, and he felt very weak. At the sound of the messenger's voice, he fainted and lay with his face to the ground. This is Daniel's account of what happened next:

> Just then a hand touched me and lifted me, still trembling, to my hands and knees. And the man said to me, "Daniel, you are very precious to God, so listen carefully to what I have to say to you. Stand up, for I have been sent to you." When

he said this to me, I stood up, still trembling. Then he said, "Don't be afraid, Daniel. Since the first day you began to pray for understanding and to humble yourself before your God, your request has been heard in heaven. I have come in answer to your prayer. But for twenty-one days the spirit prince of the kingdom of Persia blocked my way. Then Michael, one of the archangels, came to help me, and I left him there with the spirit prince of the kingdom of Persia. Now I am here to explain what will happen to your people in the future, for this vision concerns a time yet to come." (Daniel 10:10–14 NLT)

The fascinating part of this story is the reason Daniel's prayer went unanswered for twenty-one days. In the words of the ESV Reformation Study Bible, the story gives us "a glimpse of spiritual battles waged in heavenly places and affecting events on earth."[15] Commenting on the verse that reveals the twenty-one-day standoff, one writer notes, "Perhaps no single verse in the whole of the Scriptures speaks more clearly than this upon the invisible powers which rule and influence nations."[16]

To us, this is all a great mystery. Jesus, however, clearly sees the spiritual realm that is invisible to us. When the answers to our prayers are delayed, all we need to know is that Jesus has told us to persevere in prayer. He is the authority over all authorities, and the supreme power over all powers, and he surrounds us with the shield of his favor (Colossians 2:10; Psalm 5:12).

The Mystery of Abiding

Waiting is not just a part of life for freeway drivers and shoppers in Black Friday checkout lines, but for everyone on the planet. Waiting is *ubiquitous*, a word that means that something exists or is happening everywhere at the same time. So, we're all waiting, and though we're all waiting for different things, we do so for many of the same reasons. We Christ followers wait because of the same ordinary hindrances as everybody else, but we are unique in that we also wait on God. And what makes it possible for us to wait on God in continuous, uninterrupted fellowship is mysterious even to us.

In the Old Testament, the prophet Hosea urged his listeners to "wait continually for your God" (Hosea 12:6 ESV). The idea is to constantly keep turning your heart toward God. In the New Testament, Jesus said something similar, but even better: "Abide in me, and I in you" (John 15:4 ESV). *Abide* is the verb form of *abode*, which means home, the place where you live. Some Bible versions translate this word as *remain*: "Remain in me and I will remain in you" (NLT). The hearts of true believers abide in God and God abides in them as the Person of the Holy Spirit. This mutual, perpetual abiding was not possible in Hosea's day. It is only possible for us today because after Jesus returned to heaven, God sent the Holy Spirit to dwell in the hearts of believers. This is both mysterious and miraculous!

While the Spirit will never leave us (Acts 14:16), we can put our connection with God "on hold" if we choose to ignore God or rebel against him. But if we are sincerely following after God, no matter how busy our lives become, we can continually abide in, or wait upon, him. It's an attitude of the heart that we carry with us all the time. Charles Stanley called it "active stillness," quietly waiting on God even when we're busy and productive.[17] John Piper called it "a spirit of waiting in the midst of work."[18] Andrew Murray described it as "a matter of the heart, and ... what the heart is full of, occupies it, even when the thoughts are otherwise engaged." For example, he said, "A father's heart may be filled continuously with intense love and longing for a sick wife or child at a distance, even though pressing business requires all his thoughts."[19]

Forced Waiting

As we go through life abiding in God, no moment of our lives is hidden from him. If we are convinced of his sovereignty, we recognize that all of our waiting, even in the most ordinary situations, can become God's teaching or refining tool. We're often forced to wait when our day is interrupted by inconvenient, unexpected events that we can't do anything about: a backup on the freeway, the need to hear back from one person before responding to another, or a delay in our doctor's schedule. Though these delays usually resolve quickly, they can reveal our impatience (*What? I came early for my appointment and now I have to wait? Really?*). Impatience with the people and things that slow us down is, of course, ultimately impatience with God. So even our brief times of forced waiting can help us recognize the need to walk a little more surrendered to God.

Unforced Waiting

When we intentionally choose to wait or to delay gratification, it's usually because we expect that something better will, or could, happen if we wait. When we're in control of our choices and we freely choose to wait, the waiting experience may be much less stressful because it's not been forced upon us by unexpected circumstances.

We can choose to wait in the midst of the normal busy flow of life as an expression of patience and love for another person. Many who wait on God continually in the abiding sense also choose to wait on him with their physical presence, setting aside a daily time to talk to him and read the Word, maybe before or after their busy workday. Other times, we might choose to take a few hours or even a few days for a personal retreat, a time of special waiting on God before a busy season of life begins or to seek direction about an important decision.

The Mystery of the Bride

In Ephesians, Paul said, "This is a profound mystery—but I am talking about Christ and the church" (5:32). Though he was speaking about the marriage of a human couple, the mystery he mentions was about what lies ahead for us, the church. "The church" means all who have believed in Christ since the day of Pentecost in Acts 2, and the Bible says that the church (all of us) are the bride of Christ. Revelation 19 proclaims the marriage between Christ and his bride, the church. While we do not fully comprehend this mystery, as Christ's betrothed, we wait for his return.

Revelation 21 speaks not only of the bride, but also about other magnificent things we are all waiting for:

- God will make a new heaven and a new earth. The old heaven and earth will pass away, and there will no longer be any sea.

- God will live with us. We will be his people, and he will be our God.

- God will wipe every tear from our eyes and there will be no more death or mourning or crying or pain.

And that's not all! Philippians 3:21 tells us that Jesus will also "transform our lowly bodies so that they will be like his glorious body."

These events will be the grand culmination of all our waiting upon God throughout our lives. We don't know when our Bridegroom will return for us, but we know that he delays out of love, "not wanting anyone to perish, but everyone to come to repentance" (2 Peter 3:9). He told his followers to "keep watch, because you do not know on what day your Lord will come" (Matthew 24:36).

And so ... we wait!

Evil Waits Too.

> September 11, 2001, was a day of unprecedented shock and suffering in the history of the United States. The nation was unprepared. At 8:46 on the morning of September 11, 2001, the United States became a nation transformed.... More than 2,600 people died at the World Trade Center; 125 died at the Pentagon; 256 died on the four planes. The death toll surpassed that at Pearl Harbor in December 1941.
> —*The 9/11 Commission Report*[20]

In the beginning, the plan for the 9/11 attacks was called "the planes operation." The original idea was even bigger than what actually took place: ten planes would attack targets on both the east and west coasts. In late 1998 or early 1999, the planes operation idea was presented to al-Qaeda leader Osama Bin Laden, who trimmed the number of planes to four. In the fall of 1999, operatives began training for the attacks that would take place two years later.

9/11 was possible because Bin Laden had already invested a decade in methodically building a lethal infrastructure, rallying zealots to contribute money, radicalizing recruits, and "publicly declaring that it was God's decree that every Muslim should try his utmost to kill any American, military or civilian, anywhere in the world, because of American 'occupation' of Islam's holy places and aggression against Muslims."[21] On September 11, 2001 Bin Laden's years of planning and preparation bore their hateful fruit. Evil had waited until the time was right.

Evil was just as patient two thousand years ago as it is today. When Paul was in jail, his nephew found out about a plot to kill him—and it was clear that the would-be assassins didn't mind waiting until the time was right. Paul's nephew told the authorities, "Some Jews have agreed to ask you to bring Paul before the Sanhedrin tomorrow on the pretext of wanting more accurate information about him. Don't give in to them, because more than forty of them are waiting in ambush for him. They have taken an oath not to eat or drink until they have killed him. They are ready now, waiting for your consent to their request" (Acts 23:20–21). Armed with this information, the authorities transferred Paul in the dark of night to another location.

Evil waits in different ways. On one occasion when Jesus had gone to dinner at a Pharisee's home, he said some things that neither the Pharisees nor the law experts wanted to hear. The Bible reports, "When Jesus went outside, the Pharisees and the teachers of the law began to oppose him fiercely and to besiege him with questions, waiting to catch him in something he might say" (Luke 11:53–54).

Today we live in a society where evil flourishes in many forms. Paul's counsel to the early church about how to respond to evil is as helpful to us now as it was to believers in his day. In Romans 12, Paul instructs them to:

- Hate evil and instead cling to what is good.
- Never repay evil with evil when someone does you wrong.
- Not be overcome by evil, but instead overcome evil with good.

We will be able to do each of these things and respond to evil in the right way if we wait on the Lord for direction, self-control, and wisdom for every unique circumstance we face. Waiting on the Lord is never more necessary than when we're in situations that tempt us or challenge us to compromise. Sometimes it takes courage to wait on God, especially if others are pressuring us or scoffing at our resolve to wait. David waited on God even as his enemies were waiting for the chance to attack him. He spoke to God saying, "Teach me how to live, O Lord. Lead me along the right path, for my enemies are waiting for me." And then, perhaps speaking as much to himself as to the Lord, he concluded with these words:

> Wait patiently for the LORD. Be brave and courageous. Yes, wait patiently for the LORD.
> PSALM 27:11, 14 NLT

God's Best Is Worth the Wait.

For as long as we are alive, we are destined to wait. As noted previously, waiting is an unalterable part of life and, for Christ followers, it is a part of the Father's plan for making us more and more like his Son.

How can we best cooperate with God to make the very most of our times in the waiting room? Here are two final thoughts that may be helpful.

Waiting on God takes practice.

Waiting on God is a learned behavior. Because we are by nature self-centered and impatient, no one naturally waits happily for much of anything, and least of all for God. Waiting on God is a choice.

The more we comprehend that God really is the "goodest" good in the universe, and that he wants to lavish that goodness upon us, the more we become willing to bring our whole lives before him, not just asking for what we want, but asking what *he* wants *for us*. But, as has been mentioned, human nature does not typically gravitate toward God in humility until our backs are against the wall.

All of us, even sincere believers, tend to come to God with our hat in our hand only after we have come to the end of ourselves. When we are exhausted from trying to solve our intractable problems, or when we're in a desperate situation, we may finally turn to God as a last resort. And you know what? God is not one bit surprised by this. In his compassion for our fallen human nature, he waits patiently on us until we become willing to wait on him, even if it is in the midst of a dire circumstance. But it's so much better and far wiser to learn to wait on God before we're in the middle of a crisis or a catastrophe!

> Waiting on God is a choice.

Charles Stanley, who had so much wisdom about how to wait on God, offered this suggestion: "Learn to listen to God when you don't have a big issue in life, when there's no pressure. Make it a habit to listen to him with little things in life that are not so crucial at that particular point.... Listen to him when it's something simple: *Lord, would you have me to do this?*"[22] His point was that if we have learned to wait on God in little daily things, we'll know how to wait on him when we're facing big decisions and difficulties.

Be open to changing course.

When we are going the wrong way, it's often because we have not asked God for direction, or because we rejected the direction he gave us. But God knows exactly how to pull us out of the mud and mire and put our feet back on solid ground (Psalm 40:2). God never runs out of grace.

In her book, *Is That You God? A Taste of Discerning the Voice of God*, Priscilla Shirer shares a story about how God intervened to stop a mistake she was in the process of making. She wanted to enroll at Dallas Theological Seminary to earn a doctoral degree. She had filled out "mounds of paperwork," wrote essays, and gathered her references. She was so excited about moving in this new direction that she decided to drive to the seminary and deliver her application in person. She remembers, "I thought it held the key to my future." In the car, on the way to the seminary, God intervened. She recalls,

> Suddenly, I heard a quiet voice whisper to my heart, "Did you decide to go to school without consulting Me, Priscilla? More education is a good thing, Priscilla, but I don't want you back in school right now." Such authority rang in those soft-spoken words that I didn't need to question whether I was hearing from God. Though I very much wanted to pursue my dream, I immediately took the next exit and drove back home. Surprisingly, the desire to go back to school completely left me by the time I got there. Not once have I regretted the choice. Many times I've paused to thank God for it as new twists and happy surprises would've made

completing a doctorate program very difficult, if not impossible.

She tells her readers, "Know that God will send you a red flag of conviction when He wants you to 'Stop' and will send you a green light of ease and peace in your life to say, 'Go.' We don't have to wonder what God wants for us. That's why we've got to stay attuned."[23]

What God wants for us is always what's best for us, and God's best is worth waiting for!

Afterword
A Personal Note

I DID NOT REALIZE UNTIL I WAS WELL INTO WRITING this book how little I really understood about waiting on God. It was humbling to recognize that I have so often forged ahead, not waiting to see if my plan was God's plan too. I began to feel like a hypocrite: who was I to write about waiting on God when I had practiced it so little in my own life? But then, as I dug deeper into what it really means to wait on God, reading what others have written, and especially what God says about it in his Word, I began to grasp how truly awesome it is that the God of the universe wants to supernaturally and personally guide me as I journey through life. As I began to seek God in a very different way, I discovered for myself how incredibly bless-ed it is, as Andrew Murray phrased it, "when a waiting soul and a waiting God meet each other."

I'm so grateful to have had the opportunity to write this book because what I learned in the process has profoundly changed my relationship with God. I hope that reading this book has been as meaningful for you as writing it was for me.

Sola gratia,

Debbie

Resources

Books and Articles

Waiting on God by Andrew Murray (Nisbet & Co. LTD, 1896)

Is That You, God? A Taste of Discerning the Voice of God by Priscilla Shirer (LifeWay Press, 2009)

"The Names of God and Why They Matter" by David Jeremiah, davidjeremiah.org/knowgod/the-names-of-god

Videos and Music

"Waiting Here For You"

Melodie Malone at LIFT Creative Conference: youtube.com/watch?v=pHqAs5dBiOA

Martin Smith: youtube.com/watch?v=-8d80ok40TQ

Christy Nockels:
youtube.com/watch?v=J3OEGnH5x8g

"A Strange Way to Save the World"

4HIM:
youtube.com/watch?v=p__YvFbsCz4

Gateway Worship:
youtube.com/watch?v=5cNpXboJ79Y

Charles Stanley sermon, "Waiting on God's Timing"

Part 1: youtube.com/watch?v=gRs5brImLH8

Part 2: youtube.com/watch?v=XFVM43iMSGo

Charles Stanley sermon, "When God Says Wait"

youtube.com/watch?v=gygGZkMykRE

Unsure of your relationship with God? This information may help:

The 3 Circles
youtube.com/watch?v=lcj5G_4dwrI

How to Know God
cru.org/us/en/how-to-know-god.html

Acknowledgments

I am both grateful and greatly indebted to the authors, pastors, musicians, and bloggers, both living and now in the Lord's presence, whose work informed and inspired me as I researched and wrote this book. I also want to thank the many friends who encouraged me and prayed for me as this book was taking shape. Special thanks goes to Jerry and Jan Morrison, Ric and Anne Wagner, and Chris Barr for reading the manuscript and offering helpful suggestions.

Notes

1. Charles Stanley, *Life Principles Bible* (Nashville, TN: Thomas Nelson), note on Psalm 40.

2. Andrew Murray, *Waiting on God* (London: Nisbet & Co. LTD, 1896), Day 20; italics added for emphasis.

3. Murray, Day 20.

4. Murray, Day 9 and Day 13.

5. L. B. Cowman (compiler), "August 17," *Streams in the Desert* (Grand Rapids, MI: Zondervan, 1982), 241–242.

6. "What Does John 11:17 Mean?" *BibleRef.com: www.bibleref.com/John/11/John-11-17.html.*

7. Robert Jamieson, Andrew Robert Fausset, and David Brown, *Jamieson-Fausset-Brown Commentary* (Hartford, CT: S. S. Scranton & Co., 1871), John 11:25.

8. Maria Vernon Graham Havergal, *Memorials of Frances Ridley Havergal* (London: James Nisbet & Co. LTD, 1882), 95.

9. Murray, Day 20.

10. Murray, Day 24.

11. Sermon clip of T. D. Jakes in "Lessons on Forgiveness from T. D. Jakes," *Tell Me More*, NPR radio (April 5, 2012).

12 Charles Stanley, "Waiting on God's Timing, Part 2," *In Touch Ministries*: www.youtube.com/watch?v=XFVM43iMSGo.

13 Joel Stucki, "While You Wait, Do These Three Things" (June 12, 2018), *Open the Bible*: https://openthebible.org/article/while-you-wait-do-these-three-things-2/.

14 Murray, Day 12.

15 *Reformation Study Bible, English Standard Version,* ed. R. C. Sproul (Sanford, FL: Ligonier Ministries, 2010), Daniel 10:13.

16 *Ellicott's Commentary for English Readers,* ed. Charles John Ellicott (London: Cassell & Company, 1905), Daniel 10:13.

17 Charles Stanley, "Waiting on God's Timing, Part 1," *In Touch Ministries*: www.youtube.com/watch?v=gRs5brImLH8.

18 John Piper, "How do I Wait for God?" episode 1505 (July 29, 2020; original sermon date: 1982), *Desiring God*.

19 Murray, Day 30.

20 "The 9/11 Commission Report, Final Report of the National Commission on Terrorist Attacks Upon the United States, Executive Summary," *https://9-11commission.gov/report/911Report_Exec.pdf*.

21 "The 9/11 Commission Report."

22 Charles Stanley, "When God Says Wait," *In Touch Ministries*: *www.youtube.com/watch?v=gygGZkMykRE*.

23 Priscilla Shirer, *Is That You, God? A Taste of Discerning the Voice of God* (Nashville, TN: LifeWay Press, 2009).

Other Bible translations used:

Scripture quotations marked NLT are taken from the Holy Bible, New Living Translation, copyright ©1996, 2004, 2015 by Tyndale House Foundation. Used by permission of Tyndale House Publishers, Carol Stream, Illinois 60188. All rights reserved.

Scripture quotations marked ESV are from the ESV® Bible (The Holy Bible, English Standard Version®), © 2001 by Crossway, a publishing ministry of Good News Publishers. Used by permission. All rights reserved. The ESV text may not be quoted in any publication made available to the public by a Creative Commons license. The ESV may not be translated in whole or in part into any other language.

Scripture quotations marked MSG are taken from The Message, copyright © 1993, 2002, 2018 by Eugene H. Peterson. Used by permission of NavPress. All rights reserved. Represented by Tyndale House Publishers.

Emphasis added in some Scripture quotations.

About the Author

Debbie Barr is an author, health educator, and speaker with a passion for encouraging people to engage deeply with God as they journey through tough times.

She earned her bachelor's degree in journalism from the Pennsylvania State University and her master's degree in health education from East Carolina University. A master certified health education specialist (MCHES®), Debbie is especially interested in health and wellness, health literacy, and Christian growth.

She lives in Bermuda Run, North Carolina.

You can learn more about Debbie by visiting her website (debbiebarr.com), her Amazon author page (amazon.com/author/debbiebarr) or her Linkedin profile (www.linkedin.com/in/debbiebarr).

Hope and Healing

Unmasking Emotional Abuse

Six Steps to Reduce Stress

Ten Tips for Parenting the Smartphone Generation

Five Keys to Dealing with Depression

Seven Answers for Anxiety

Five Keys to Raising Boys

Freedom From Shame

Five Keys to Health and Healing

When a Loved One Is Addicted

Social Media and Depression

Rebuilding Trust after Betrayal

How to Deal with Toxic People

The Power of Connection

Why Failure Is Never Final

Find Your Purpose in Life

Here Today, Ghosted Tomorrow

Caregiving

Forgiveness

The Mystery of Waiting

Overwhelmed

www.hendricksonrose.com